Frances Turnbull

All maps are derived from OpenStreetMap.org. OpenStreetMap is open data, licensed under the Open Data Commons Open Database License (ODbL). They are made available by MapCruzin.com, free to copy, distribute and adapt as required.

Celebration! Song Book

Musicaliti Publishing, Bolton, UK

ISBN: 978-1907935831

www.musicaliti.co.uk

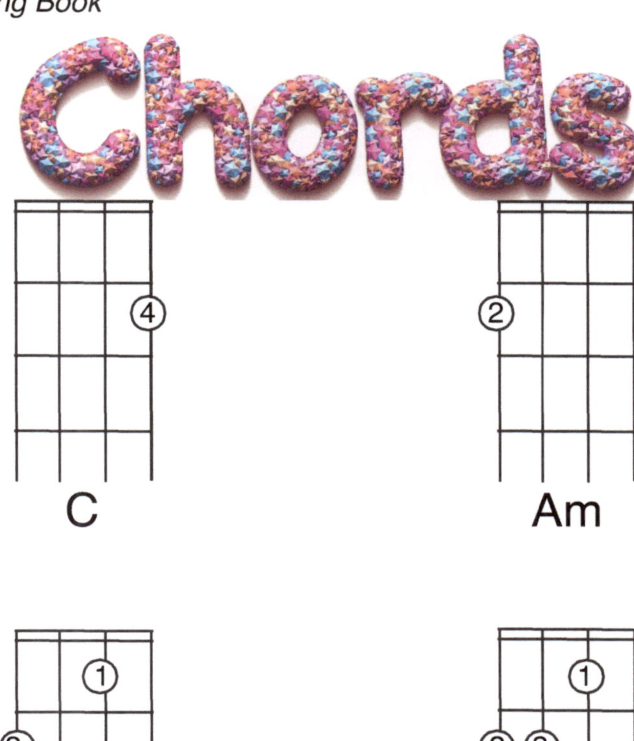

Ukuleles are small, accessible and relatively cheap instruments that can be used to play the accompaniment to many songs.

Each string should be tuned to specific notes (can be found on tuned instruments like xylophones, pianos or recorders etc.). The standard ukulele tuning is:

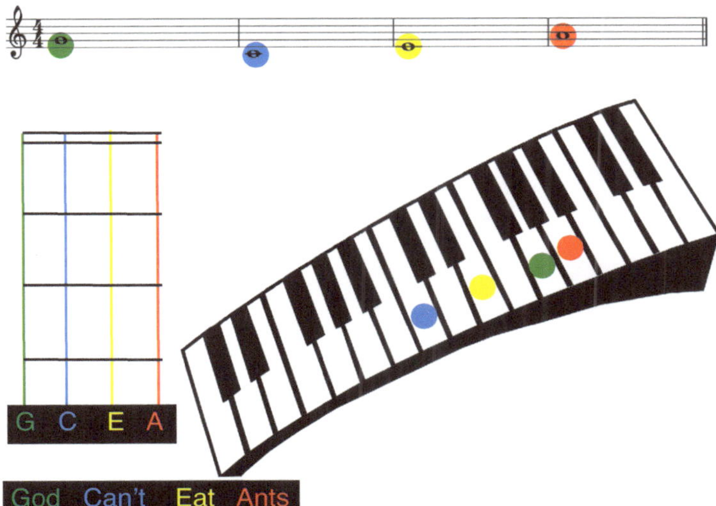

By placing your fingers on the frets at the positions on the pictures, (between the lines), you change the sound of the strings into chords when strummed altogether.

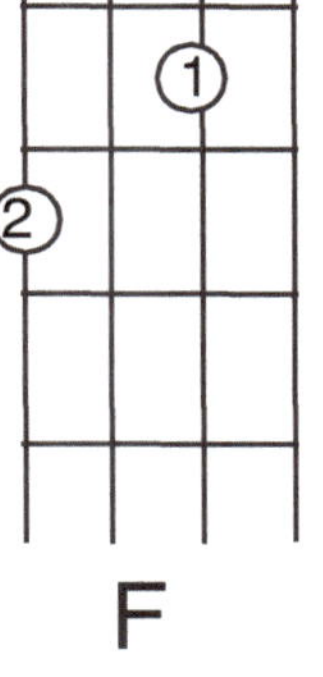

1
2 3
Dm

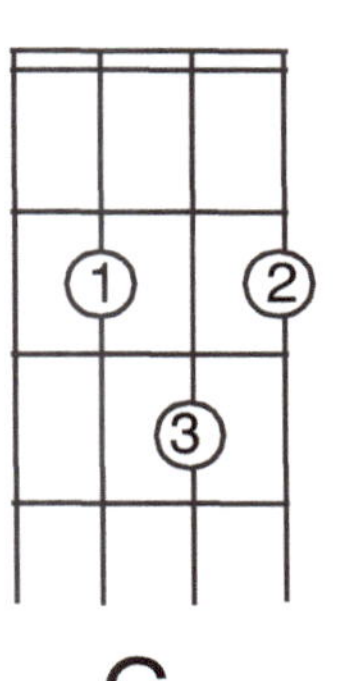

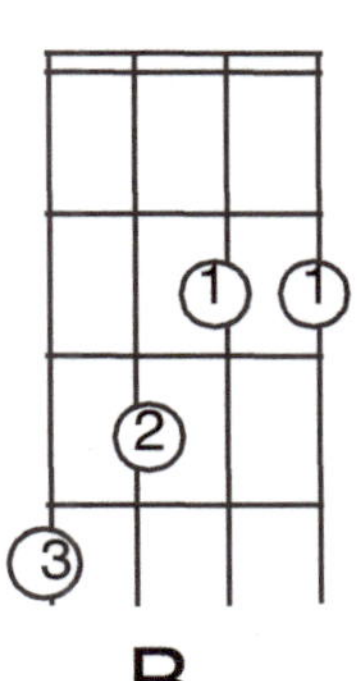

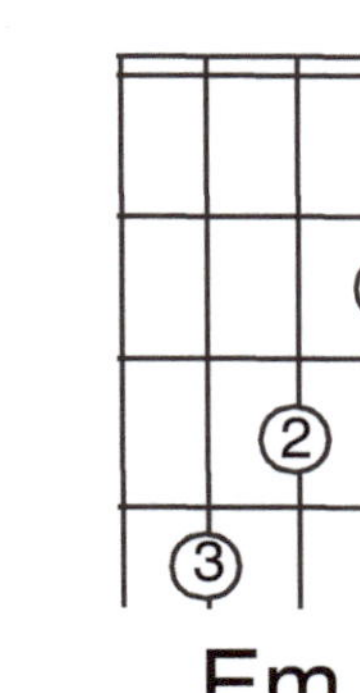

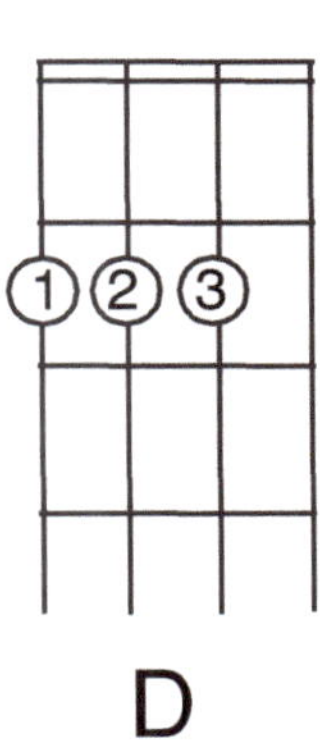

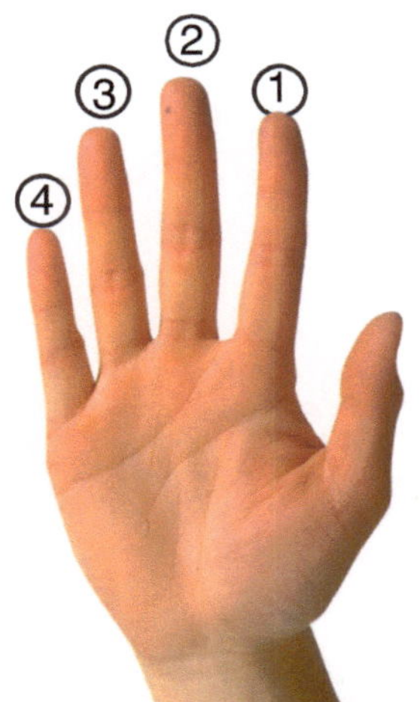

Party
вечеринка
מפלגה
partido
Partí
جشن
Musicaliti

COUNTRY: Iran

WHAT is the holiday called?
Čahāṛ Šanbé Sūrī - pronounced Chahar Shanbeh Soori

WHEN is it?
Last Wednesday of the Iranian year

WHAT is it for?
It is the Iranian New Year, and it means "Red Wednesday".

WHAT do people do:
People light bonfires in public places to wish everyone good luck and happiness.

Celebration! Song Book
Festival of Fire
F Turnbull
Am
In I - ran, o - ver fire,
2
Em
wea - ring masks, door-to-door,
3
Dm
gi - ving wa - ter,
4
Em
Am
gi - ving gieel.
usicaliti
9

HOW do people from Iran celebrate?

People jump over flames of a fire and say:
"Sorkhi-ye to az man; Zardi-ye man az to"

It means:
"Give me your beautiful red colour; take away my poorly yellow colour"

What else do people do?

- Jump over flames
- Give each other nuts and berries, called gieel
- Give each other buckets of water

Pumpkin Pumpkin

Traditional

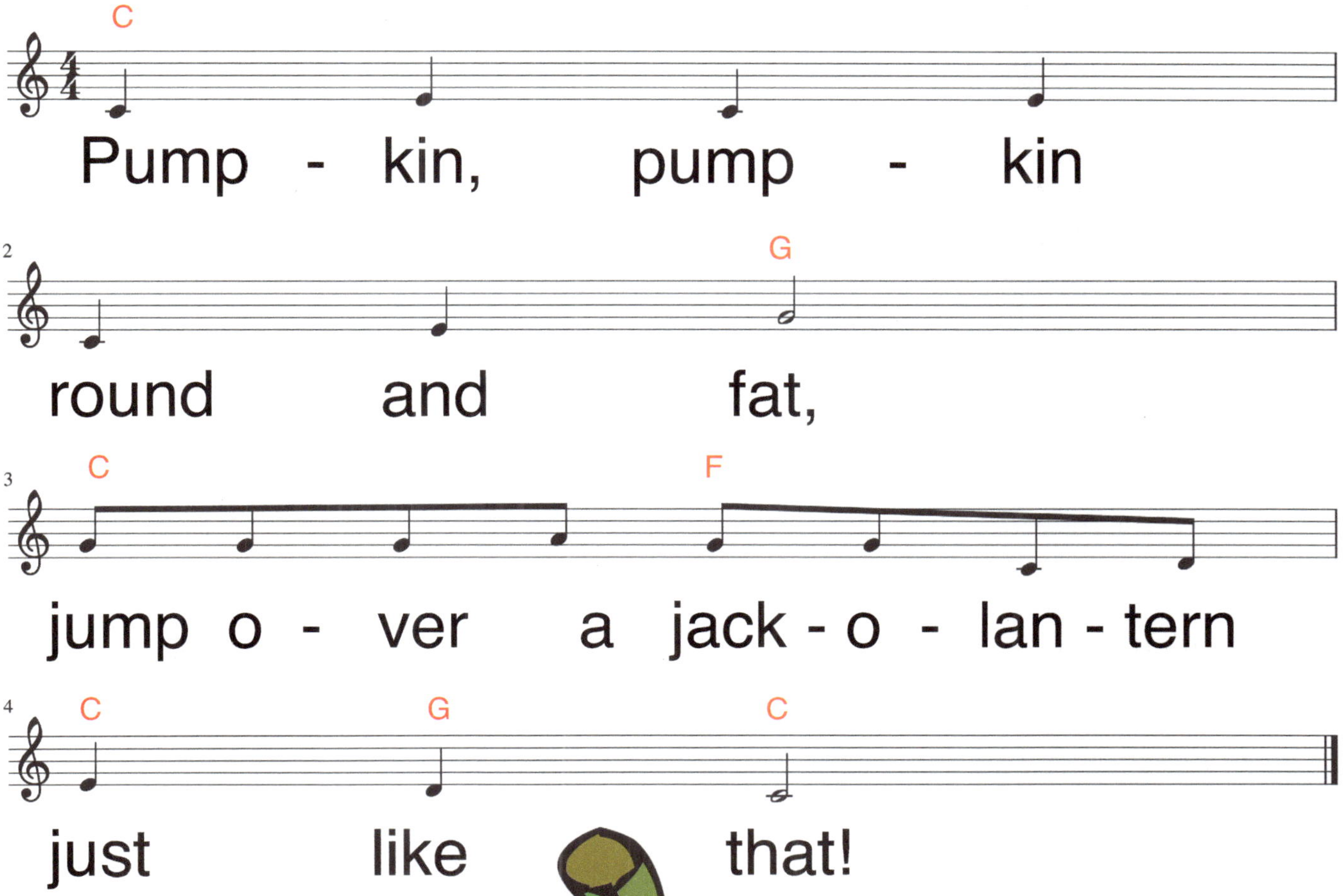

C

Pump - kin, pump - kin

2 G

round and fat,

3 C F

jump o - ver a jack - o - lan - tern

4 C G C

just like that!

COUNTRY: United States of America

WHAT is the holiday called:
Independence Day

WHEN is it:
4th of July

WHAT is it for:
It is the day that America became its own country, not owned by England.

WHAT do people do:
People meet up with family and friends, go to concerts and ceremonies about the history of the country.

Independence Day

F Turnbull

It's In - de - pen - dence Day,

Fi-re-work par- ty for all to - day,

5 C

It's In - de - pen - dence Day,

Fi-re-work par- ty for all to - day!

HOW do people from America celebrate?

This is a very important day for people to remember the history of the country, so school children have special assemblies where they act out what happened a long time ago and sing songs. Government people also give a lot of speeches.

People sometime organise funny competitions, like who can eat the most hotdogs!

What else do people do?

- Play baseball
- Hold parades
- Family barbeques

Simple Simon

Traditional

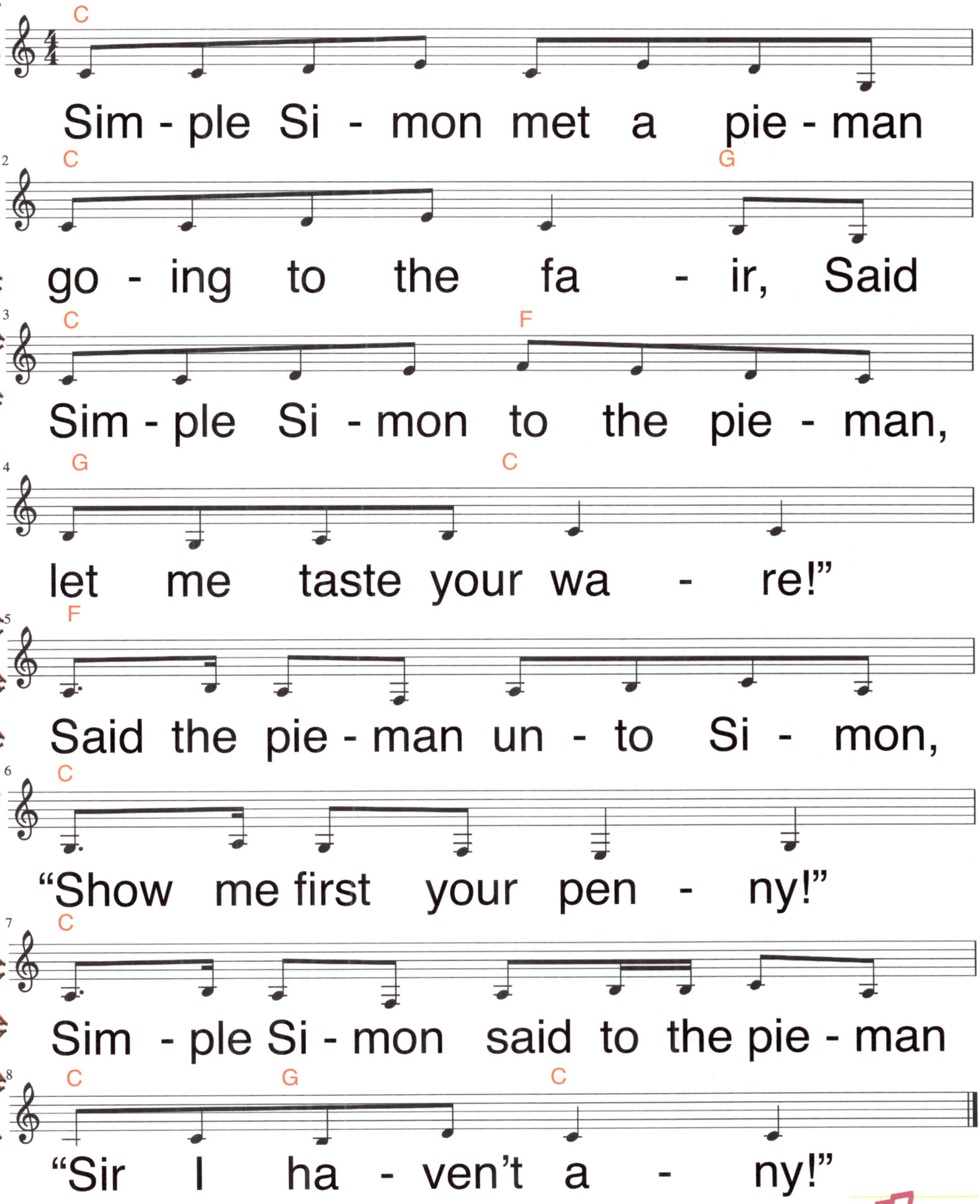

C
Sim - ple Si - mon met a pie - man

2 C G
go - ing to the fa - ir, Said

3 C F
Sim - ple Si - mon to the pie - man,

4 G C
let me taste your wa - re!"

5 F
Said the pie - man un - to Si - mon,

6 C
"Show me first your pen - ny!"

7 C
Sim - ple Si - mon said to the pie - man

8 C G C
"Sir I ha - ven't a - ny!"

Frances Turnbull

China

COUNTRY: China

WHAT is the holiday called?
Spring Festival - or 春节 (Chūn Jié)

WHEN is it?
It changes every year, depending on the moon, so is sometimes called Lunar New Year.

WHAT is it for?
It is a time to forgive and to wish everyone good luck.

WHAT do people do:
People clean their houses to sweep away bad luck and make space for good luck.

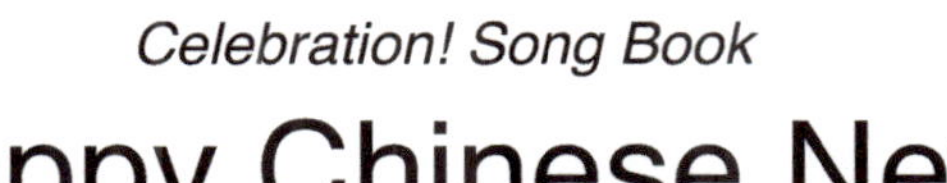

Happy Chinese New Year

F Turnbull

HOW do people from China celebrate?

People usually have a 7 day holiday where they see family, give presents like red envelopes with money, and put up a lot of colourful decorations and get new clothes. They have a big dinner, stay up late on the night before, and have fireworks.

Many decorations include dragons and lions to wis people strength.

What else do people do?

- Clean houses
- Red envelopes of money
- Decorate with pictures of lions and dragons

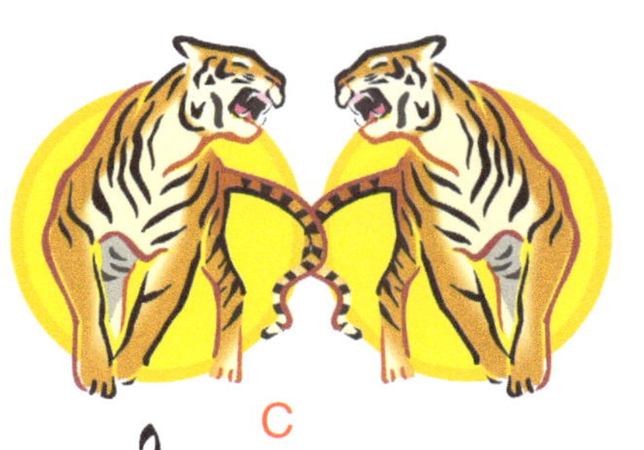

Two Little Tigers

两只老虎

Traditional

两 只 老 虎 两 只 老 虎

Liang shj louw haw, Liang shj louw haw

Two little ti - gers, two little ti - gers

跑 得 快 跑 得 快

Pow der quay Pow der quay

Run-ning fast Run-ning fast

一 只 没 有 耳 朵 一 只 没 有 尾 巴

Ee shj may yo ar doo Ee shj may yo way bah

One has no ears, One has no tail

真 奇 怪 真 奇 怪

Jen tsi quay, Jen tsi quay

See how strange! See how strange!

Frances Turnbull

COUNTRY: South Africa

WHAT is the holiday called?
Reed Ceremony - or UmKhosi Womhlanga

WHEN is it?
The second week in September.

WHAT is it for?
To show that girls and ladies will build the Zulu nation.

WHAT do people do:
Dance and give reeds to the King of KwaZulu.

Reed Dance

F Turnbull

C G
King of Zu - lu's

2 F C
has a par - ty

3 C G
e - very year Sep -

4 F C
tem - ber time!

HOW do people from South Africa celebrate?

The older women teach the teenage girls about Zulu history and traditions. The teenage girls learn dances in traditional costumes and present reeds to the King, to show that they will build the Zulu nation.

Traditional clothes include beautiful bead jewellery and wearing animal skins, dancing to drum music.

What else do people do?

- Collect reeds
- Traditional dances
- Beadwork jewellery

In the Jungle

Traditional

C F

In the jun-gle, the migh-ty jun- gle, the

3 C G

li - on sleeps to - night,

5 C F

In the jun-gle, the migh-ty jun- gle, the

7 C G

li - on sleeps to - night,

9 C F

Eeee - ee - ee - ee -

11 C G

Ee, a-wum-ba-weh

13 C F

Eeee - ee - ee - ee -

15 C G

Ee, a-wum-ba-weh

Frances Turnbull

Alaska

STATE: Alaska (in the United States of America)

WHAT is the holiday called?
Spring Whale Festival - or Naluqatak

WHEN is it?
In the spring.

WHAT is it for?
To celebrate the success of the fisherman.

WHAT do people do:
Sing and dance, while they get the food that the fishermen have caught.

Naluqatak

F Turnbull

Am
Na-lu- qa-tak, na-lu- qa-tak,

3 Dm
Whale par-ty, whale par-ty,

5 Am
Peo-ple jum-ping, peo-ple jum-ping

7 Dm
On a seal skin, on a seal skin!

HOW do people from Alaska celebrate?

People from all the villages get together and have a prayer of thanks for the fisherman who have provided for them, especially the captains. Then they raise the ship flags and have traditional food, like goose, caribou (reindeer), seals, and whales. Then they dance to drum music and singing.

They used to make trampolines of animal skins!

What else do people do?

- Seal blanket toss
- Goose soup
- Dressing up

My Paddle

Traditional

Am
My pad - dle's keen and bright,

2 Am
Fla - shing like sil - ver,

3 Am
Fol - low the wild goose flight

4 Am
Dip, dip, and swing!

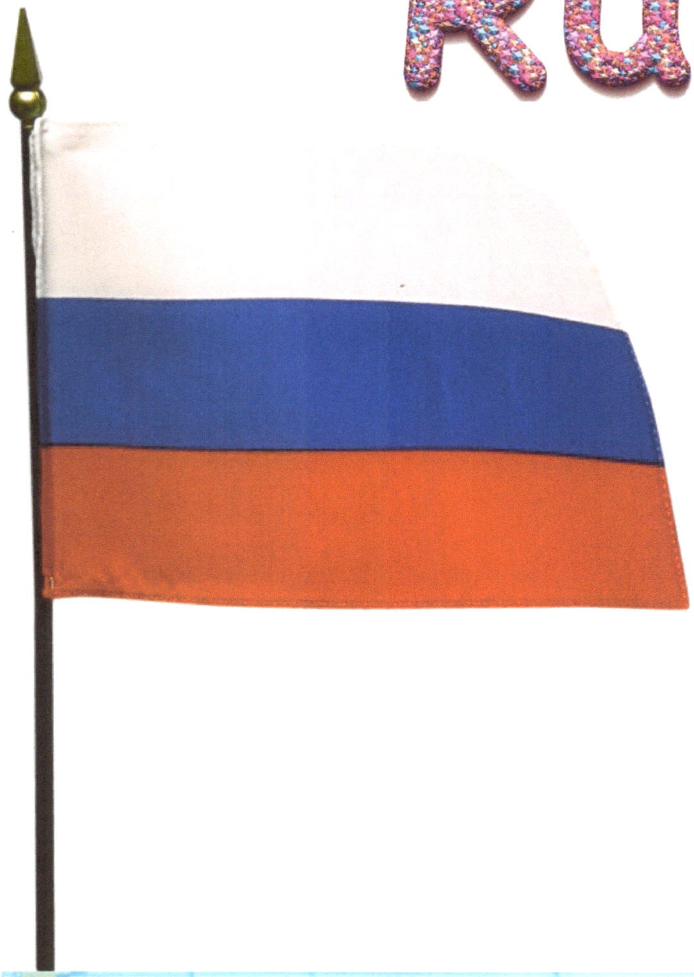

COUNTRY: Russia

WHAT is the holiday called?
Pancake Week - or Maslenitsa

WHEN is it?
The seventh week before Easter.

WHAT is it for?
To celebrate Great Lent.

WHAT do people do:
People use up all their meat, butter, milk and eggs.

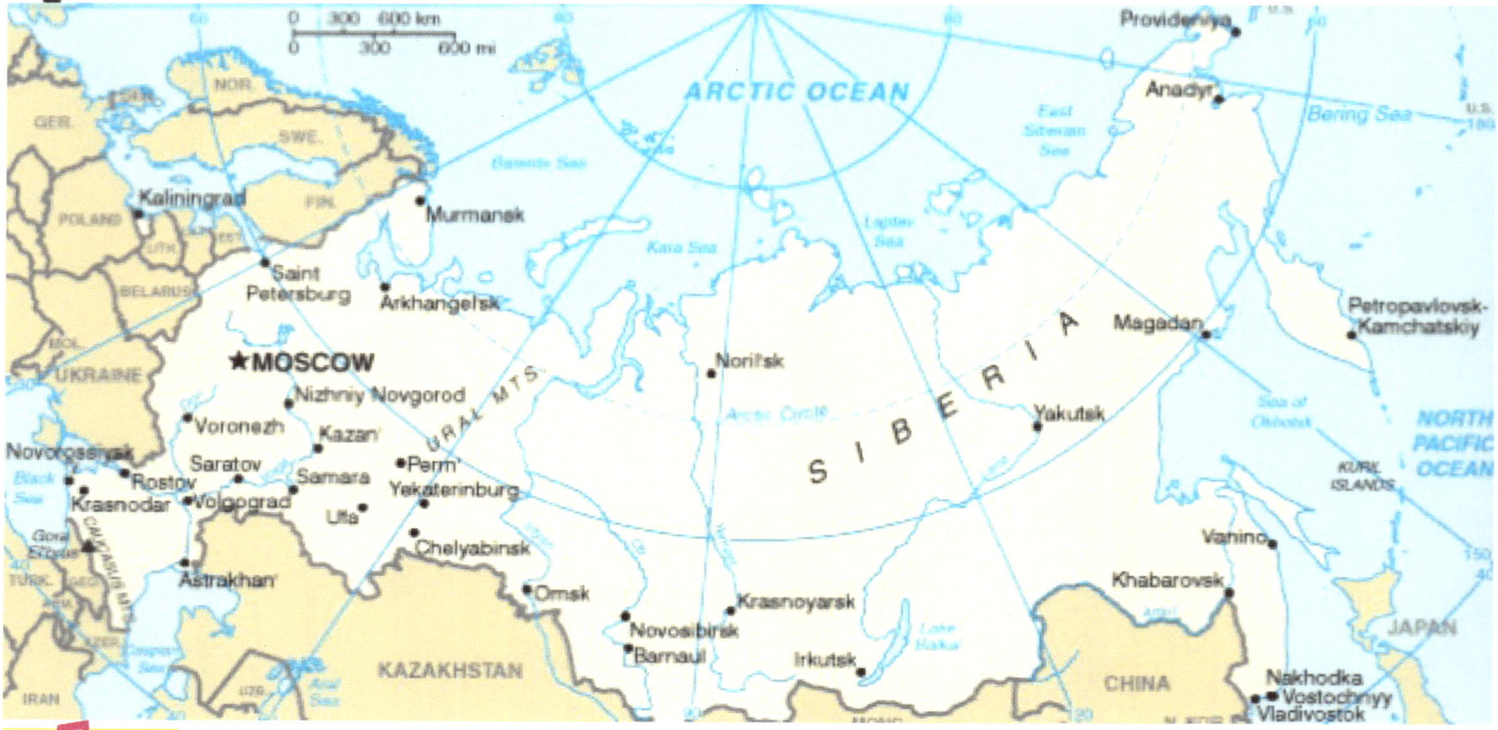

Pancake Week

F Turnbull

HOW do people from Russia celebrate?

This is the last party that people can have before Easter, so use up all their tasty food. Some people have rules about different people they have to visit in the week. They are also not allowed to have music and dancing.

People have special days called Forgiveness Sunday and Clean Monday.

What else do people do?

- Masquerades
- Snowball fights
- Pillow fights

Mummy Loves

Traditional

C

Mum-my loves and Dad - dy loves and

3 C

everybody loves little ba - by,

C

Bro-ther loves and sis - ter loves and

7 C

everybody loves little ba - by!

COUNTRY: Israel

WHAT is the holiday called?
Passover - or Pesach

WHEN is it?
Spring!

WHAT is it for?
To remember the story of Exodus in the Bible.

WHAT do people do:
People eat bread that is flat and has not had time to rise.

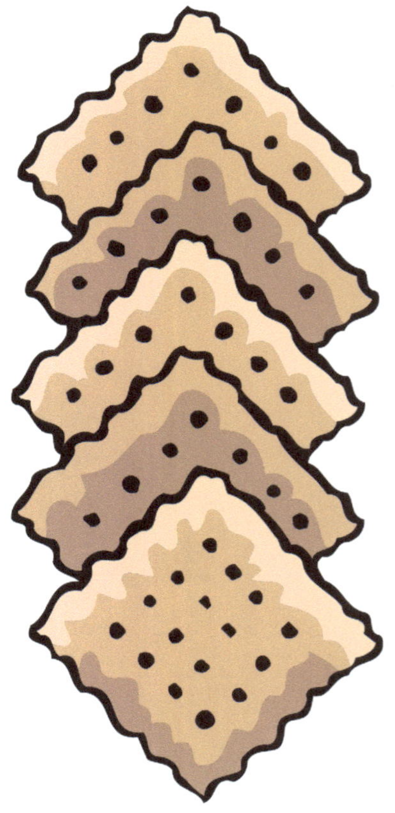

Pesach

F Turnbull

Am
Pe - sach is the

2 F
Pass - o - ver,

3 Am
Throw a - way all the

4 G
yeast and bread!

HOW do people from Israel celebrate?

People clean their houses to remember the Exodus of the Jewish people in the Bible. They throw away anything with yeast like bread or beer, and even use new pots, stoves or dishwashers that have never had yeast near them!

People also eat lamb, but must finish it that night, to remember how quickly people left in the Exodus.

What else do people do?

- Matzo bread and maror
- Celery in water
- Family reunions

Zum Gali Gali

Traditional

Dm

Zum ga-li ga-li ga-li, zum ga-li ga - li,

3 Dm

zum ga-li ga-li ga-li, zum ga-li ga - li,

5 Dm

He-cha-lutz le' man a - vo - dah,

7 Dm

A-vo-dah le' man he-cha-lutz,

9 Dm

He-cha-lutz le' man a - vo - dah,

11 Dm

A-vo-dah le' man he-cha-lutz!

Frances Turnbull

United Kingdom

COUNTRY: ENGLAND

WHAT IS THE HOLIDAY CALLED:
St George's Day

WHEN IS IT:
23 April

WHY DO WE HAVE IT:
In tradition, St George slayed a dragon and protected a lot people. He was actually killed for his belief in God in 303AD.

HOW DO WE CELEBRATE IT:
People used to wear a red rose in their lapel. Today we put the English flag up. Churches usually sing Jerusalem on this day.

COUNTRY: IRELAND

WHAT IS THE HOLIDAY CALLED:
St Patrick's Day

WHEN IS IT:
17 March

WHY DO WE HAVE IT:
St Patrick was kidnapped from England and taken to Ireland. After he escaped and went back to England, he became a Christian and went back to Ireland to tell people about God.

HOW DO WE CELEBRATE IT:
This day has been celebrated since the 17th century and is celebrated for being the end of Lent.

COUNTRY: SCOTLAND

WHAT IS THE HOLIDAY CALLED:
St Andrew's Day

WHEN IS IT:
5 November

WHY DO WE HAVE IT:
In the Bible, Saint Andrew introduced his brother, the Apostle Peter, to Jesus as the Messiah.

HOW DO WE CELEBRATE IT:
Since approximately 1034AD, people have celebrated St Andrew's day is celebrated with ceilidhs and dancing with swords.

COUNTRY: WALES

WHAT IS THE HOLIDAY CALLED:
St David's Day

WHEN IS IT:
1 March

WHY DO WE HAVE IT:
St David was a famous teacher from Wales, founding 12 monasteries and people have celebrated the day of his death since 1120.

HOW DO WE CELEBRATE IT:
In the past, people used to bake special biscuits, but today people celebrate by having concerts. Children take part in singing festivals, eisteddfodau, wearing leeks or daffodils on their lapels.

Saints Song

F Turnbull | F Turnbull

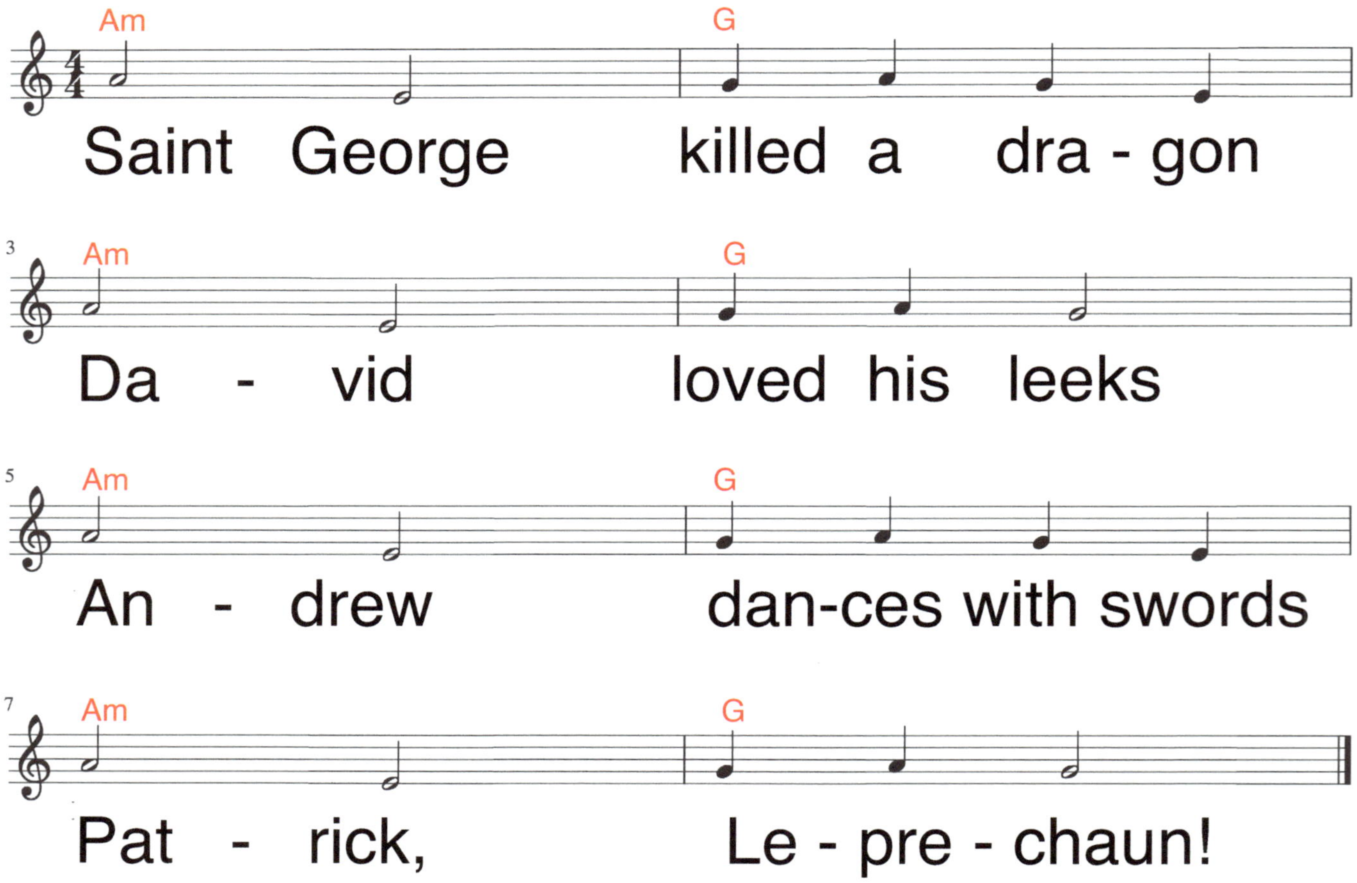

Am | G

Saint George | killed a dra - gon

3 Am | G

Da - vid | loved his leeks

5 Am | G

An - drew | dan-ces with swords

7 Am | G

Pat - rick, | Le - pre - chaun!

Greensleeves

A-las my lo-ve you do me wrong to

cast me off so dis - cour-teous-ly, for

I have lo - ved you well and lo-ng, de-

light - ing i - n your com - pa - ny,

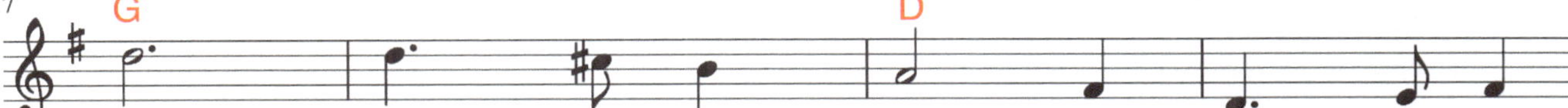

Green - sleeves was all my j - o - y,

Green - slee - ves was my de - light,

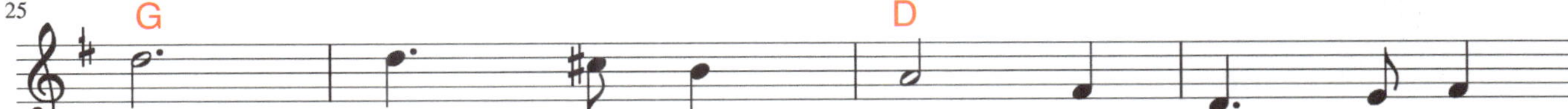

Green-sleeves was my heart of go - ld and

who but my la - dy Green - sleeves.

COUNTRY: Australia

WHAT is the holiday called?
Corroboree - or Aborigine Ceremony

WHEN is it?
At special occasions.

WHAT is it for?
To tell stories through dance.

WHAT do people do:
Play music and dance in celebration of special occasions.

HOW do people from Australia celebrate?

People believe that important spirits used to walk around the earth and create special places, which was called The Dreaming. When they have special occasions, they explain them through song and dance to do with The Dreaming.

People paint their entire bodies with paint to help to tell stories as they dance and sing.

What else do people do?

- Body painting
- Dancing
- Dressing up

Frances Turnbull

Waltzing Mathilda

Traditional

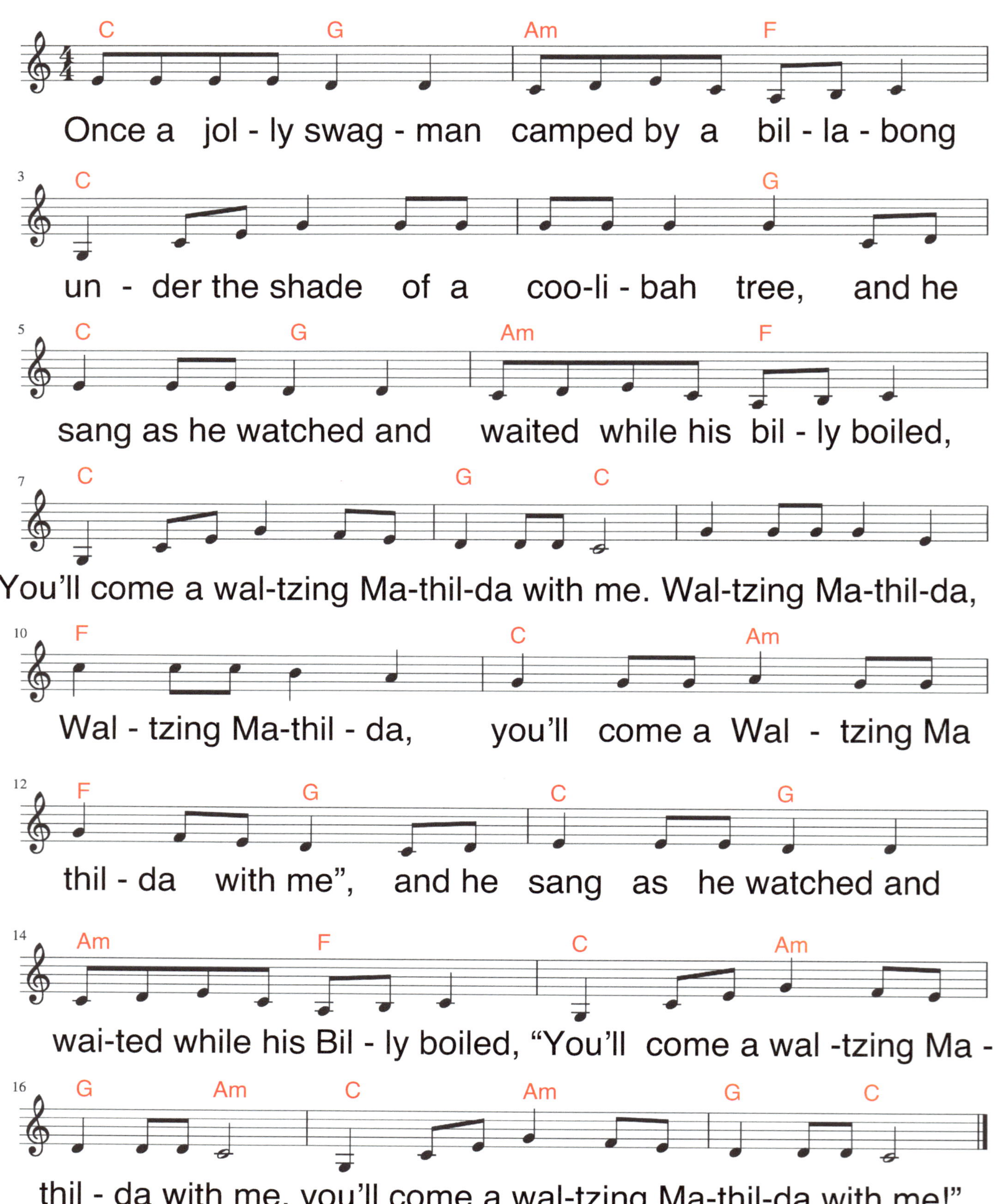

usicaliti

COUNTRY: BRAZIL

WHAT IS THE HOLIDAY CALLED:
Carnival

WHEN IS IT:
46 days in Lent, before Easter, in February

WHY DO WE HAVE IT:
To prepare for Easter

HOW DO WE CELEBRATE IT:
Wearing bright clothes, not eating meat or chicken

Frances Turnbull

Carnival

F Turnbull

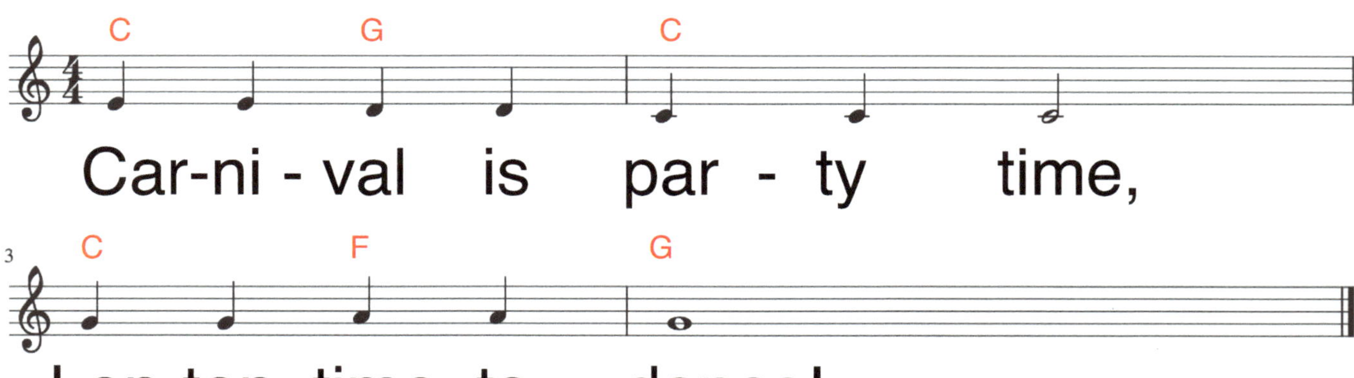

What do people from Brazil do?

People hold a parade with no meat or chicken, in February, before Lent.

They say goodbye to bad things and stop doing naughty things so that they can think about Easter time and the story of Jesus.

What else do people do?

- Hold parades
- Dance the Samba
- Wear colourful clothes

Frances Turnbull

Cho-co-la-te

Traditional

U-no, dos, tres cho, u-no, dos, tres, co,

U-no, dos, tres la, u-no, dos, tres, te,

Cho-co-la-te,cho-co-la-te, ba-te,ba-te,cho-co-la-te

Song pictures

Copy or cut out these pictures and / or rhythms to place on the stave on page 51 to write your own song!

Song pictures

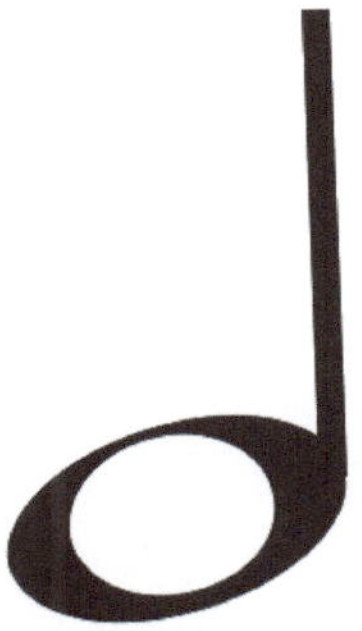

Copy or cut out these pictures and / or rhythms to place on the stave on page 51 to write your own song!

Now use the music or pictures from the previous pages to make up your own song!

The end

Have you seen our other books?

Music Gone Wild Song Book:
Animal Songs for Ukulele
ISBN 9781907935688

Musical Munchies Song Book:
Food Songs for Ukulele
ISBN 9781907787

Magical Musical Kingdom Song Book:
Magical Songs for Ukulele
ISBN 9781907935770

Goodies for Guitar:
90 songs for beginners
ISBN 9781907935695

Goodies for Guitar: Lvl 1
18 songs for beginners
ISBN 9781907935701

Goodies for Guitar: Lvl 2
20 songs for beginners
ISBN 9781907935718

Sharks, Fish, Shells
Music sessions for 2-4s
ISBN 9781907935633

Yum Yum Yum
Music sessions for 2s-4s
ISBN 9781907935206

Magical Musical Kingdom
Music sessions for 2s-4s
ISBN 9781907935152

FIND US ON:   

www.ingramcontent.com/pod-product-compliance
Lightning Source LLC
LaVergne TN
LVHW070150110826
845147LV00002B/364

* 9 7 8 1 9 0 7 9 3 5 8 3 1 *